GOD'S
Little Treasury of
VIRTUES

Unless otherwise indicated, all Scripture quotations are taken from the *New King James Version* of the Bible. Copyright © 1983, 1985, 1990 by Thomas Nelson, Inc., Nashville, Tennessee.

Verses marked KJV are taken from the *King James Version* of the Bible.

Verses marked NASB are taken from the *New American Standard Bible.* Copyright © 1960,1962, 1963,1968,1971,1972,1977 by The Lockman Foundation, LaHabra, California.

Verses marked NIV are taken from *The Holy Bible: New International Version.* Copyright © 1973, 1978, 1984 by The International Bible Society. Used by permission of Zondervan Bible Publishers.

Verses marked TLB are taken from *The Living Bible.* Copyright © 1971,1988 by Tyndale House Publishers, Inc., Wheaton, Illinois.

2nd Printing
Over 25,000 in Print

God's Little Treasury of Virtues
ISBN 1-56292-086-3
Copyright © 1996 by Honor Books, Inc.
P.O. Box 55388
Tulsa, OK 74155

Introduction

Virtue, by biblical definition, is the "fruit of the Holy Spirit" evident in our lives. We are "good" when we bear these hallmark qualities of the Spirit within us and manifest them daily to those around us. Again, the specific qualities are listed in Scripture as love, joy, peace, patience, kindness, goodness, faithfulness, gentleness, and self-control. These traits are not something that a person owns; they are something a person *does*.

In other words, *Love* is not only a quality, but an action. The person who has love in his heart shows love through generous giving. *Joy* manifests itself in praise and in voicing words of encouragement to others. *Peace* manifests itself in calmness and an even temperament. And so forth.

God's Little Treasury of Virtues is a smaller, portable version of *God's Treasury of Virtues*. You will find inspirational quotes from men and women of God who have written about what true virtue is and where it comes from. They will inspire you to walk in these godly virtues, displaying them in your everyday actions. More than anything else, virtues are manifestations to the world of the righteousness of Jesus Christ. They emanate from a heart filled with and changed by the Word of God and the Holy Spirit.

Use this book as a daily devotional, or read the entries aloud to your spouse or children. You will be built up in the virtues God has given you and be a light to your world.

LOVE

Love is Blind

*"Above all things have fervent love among
yourselves, for 'love will cover
a multitude of sins.'"*

—1 Peter 4:8
HOLY BIBLE

The First Thing

But the fruit of the Spirit is love, joy, peace, longsuffering, gentleness, goodness, faith, meekness, temperance: against such there is no law.

—Galatians 5:22-23 KJV
HOLY BIBLE

Love is Central

The fruit of the Spirit begins with love. There are nine graces spoken of, and of these nine Paul puts love at the head of the list; love is the first thing, the first in that precious cluster of fruit. Someone has said that all the other eight can be put in terms of love. Joy is love exulting; peace is love in repose; longsuffering is love on trial; gentleness is love in society; goodness is love in action; faith is love on the battlefield; meekness is love at school; and temperance is love in training...If we only just brought forth the fruit of the Spirit, what a world we would have! Men would have no desire to do evil.

—Dwight L. Moody

The D.L. Moody Year Book
selected by Emma Moody Fitt
New York: Fleming H. Revell Company, 1900

Unchanging

Love is not love
Which alters when it
alterations finds.

—Shakespeare

Sonnet CXVI
Harper's Quotations

Love and God's Will

The Will as Love

Our love of God must not be gauged by the passing feelings we experience that are not controlled by the will, but rather we must judge them by the enduring quality of the will itself. For loving God means that we join our will to God's will. It means that our will consents to whatever the will of God commands. It means that we have only one reason for wishing anything, and the reason is that we know that God wills it.

On Love of God

"Thou shalt love the Lord thy God with thy whole heart, with thy whole soul and with thy whole mind." This is the commandment of the great God, and He cannot command the impossible. Love is a fruit in season at all times, and within reach of every hand. Anyone may gather it and no limit is set.

—Mother Teresa

Malcolm Muggeridge
Something Beautiful for God
San Francisco: Harper & Row, 1971

It's a Miracle

This is the miracle that happens every time to those who really love: the more they give, the more they possess of that precious, nourishing love from which flowers and children have their strength and which could help all human beings if they would take it without doubting.

—Rainer Maria Rilke

The Book of Unusual Quotations
Selected and Edited by Rudolf Flesch
New York: Harper and Brothers Publishers, 1957

God's Love of Man

God loves you. You're rebellious, you cheat, you commit immorality, you're selfish, you sin, but God loves you with an intensity beyond anything that I could describe to you. He loves you, and He loves you so much that He gave His only Son, Jesus Christ to die on that cross; and the thing that kept Christ on that cross was love, not the nail.

—Billy Graham

The Quotable Billy Graham
Compiled and Edited by Cort R. Flint and the Staff of *Quote*
Anderson, S.C.: Droke House, 1966

The Love of Christ

Here is love, that God sent His Son, His Son who never offended, His Son who was always His delight. Herein is love, that He sent Him to save sinners; to save them by bearing their sins, by bearing their curse, by dying their death, and by carrying their sorrows.

Here is love, in that while we were yet enemies, Christ died for us; yes, here is love, in that while we were yet without strength, Christ died for the ungodly.

—John Bunyan

Titled "The Heavenly Footman" first delivered in 1698
The World's Famous Orations
Edited by William Jennings Polyan
Funk and Wagnalls Co., 1906

Christian Love

[A Christian's love] is in itself generous and disinterested; springing from no view of advantage to himself, from no regard to profit or praise—no, nor even the pleasure of loving. This is the daughter, not the parent, of his affection. By experience he knows that social love, if it means the love of our neighbor, is absolutely different from self-love, even of the most allowable kind—just as different as the objects at which they point. And yet it is sure that, if they are under due regulations, each will give additional force to the other till they mix together never to be divided.

—John Wesley

Letters: "To Dr. Conyers Middleton"
From *John Wesley's Theology*, Vol. II, p. 377, by Burtner and Chiles.
Reprinted by permission of the publisher, Abingdon Press.

For Love, For Love

Father of spirits, this my sovereign plea
I bring again and yet again to Thee.
Fulfill me now with love, that I may know
A daily inflow, daily overflow.
For love, for love, my Lord was crucified,
With cords of love He bound me to His side.
Pour through me now; I yield myself to Thee,
O Love that led my Lord to Calvary.

—Amy Carmichael

The Harper Collins Book of Prayers-
A Treasury of Prayers Through the Ages
Compiled by Robert Van de Weyer
San Francisco: Harper, 1993

Second-Century Christians

They love one another. They never fail to help widows; they save orphans from those who would hurt them. If they have something they give freely to the man who has nothing; if they see a stranger, they take him home, and are happy, as though he were a real brother. They don't consider themselves brothers in the usual sense, but brothers instead through the Spirit, in God.

— *Aristides describing Christians to the Emperor Hadria*

Best Love

Love sought is good, but giv'n
unsought is better.

—William Shakespeare

Twelfth Night, Ib. [170]

Love Just Because

We ought to love our Maker
for His own sake, without either hope
of good or fear of pain.

—Cervantes

The Book of Unusual Quotations
Selected and edited by Rudolf Flesch
New York: Harper and Brothers Publishers, 1957

More Love

Lord, it is my chief complaint;
That my love is weak and faint;
Yet I love thee and adore,
Oh for grace to love thee more!

—William Cowper

Olney Hymns, Ib
The Oxford University Press
Dictionary of Quotations, 22nd edition
New York: Crescent Books, 1985

Love Comes Back

Life may change, but it may fly not;
Hope may vanish, but can die not;
Truth be veiled, but still it burneth;
Love repulsed, but it returneth!

—*Percy Bysshe Shelley*

Hellas, l. 34
The Oxford University Press
Dictionary of Quotations, 22nd edition
New York: Crescent Books, 1985

Love and God's Favor

As long as anyone has the means
of doing good to his neighbors,
and does not do so, he shall be reckoned
a stranger to the love of the Lord.

—Irenaeus

JOY

---

*"Let all those rejoice who put their trust in You;
let them ever shout for joy, because You defend
them; let those also who love Your name
be joyful in You."*

—Psalm 5:11
HOLY BIBLE

His Blessing of Joy

O GOD, in mercy bless us; let your face beam with joy as you look down at us. Send us around the world with the news of your saving power and your eternal plan for all mankind. How everyone throughout the earth will praise the Lord! How glad the nations will be, singing for joy because you are their King and will give true justice to their people! Praise God, O world! May all the peoples of the earth give thanks to you. For the earth has yielded abundant harvests. God, even our own God, will bless us. And peoples from remotest lands will worship him.

—Psalm 67 TLB
HOLY BIBLE

Happiness or Joy?

The service of the Holy Spirit is that He helps us to distinguish pleasure from happiness and develop real joy. There are many experiences which give us temporary pleasure but do not add up to abiding satisfaction. Their thrills pass quickly, and sometimes leave a trail of regret and remorse. Some of our sense pleasures are like lightning flashes, while true joy is like the sunlight.

—Ralph W. Sockman, D.D.

From *How To Believe*
by Ralph W. Sockman, D.D.
Copyright © 1953 by Ralph W. Sockman.
Used by permission of Doubleday,
A division of Bantam Doubleday Dell Publishing Group, Inc.

Joy-Full

Jesus said to His disciples:

"If you keep My commandments, you will abide in My love, just as I have kept My Father's commandments and abide in His love. These things I have spoken to you, that My joy may remain in you, and that your joy may be full."

—John 15:10-11
HOLY BIBLE

Bitter to Sweet

The joy of life is living it and doing things of worth,
In making bright and fruitful all the barren spots of earth.
In facing odds and mastering them and rising from defeat,
And making true what once was false,
and what was bitter, sweet.
For only he knows perfectly joy whose little bit of soil
Is richer ground than what it was when he began to toil.

—Anonymous

A Treasury of Contentment
Compiled and Edited by Ralph L. Woods
New York: Trident Press, 1969
A Division of Simon and Schuster

Joyful Praise

HALLELUJAH! YES, PRAISE THE LORD!

Praise him in his Temple, and in the heavens he made with mighty power. Praise him for his mighty works. Praise his unequaled greatness. Praise him with the trumpet and with lute and harp. Praise him with the tambourines and processional. Praise him with stringed instruments and horns. Praise him with the cymbals, yes, loud clanging cymbals. Let everything alive give praises to the Lord! You praise him! Hallelujah!

—Psalm 150 TLB
HOLY BIBLE

Unconditional Joy

I know not how God will dispose of me.
I am always happy. All the world suffers;
and I, who deserve the severest discipline,
feel joys so continual and so great
that I can scarce contain them.

—Brother Lawrence

Joy's Source

Joy is like a well containing sweet water. It is not enough to know the water is there or even to drill the well. If the well is to be useful, the water must be brought to the surface. Those who know Christ have found the source of joy.

—Ron Hembree

Fruits of the Spirit
Grand Rapids, Mich.: Baker Book House, 1969

Set the Right Goal

Joy is the effect which comes when we use our powers. Joy, rather than happiness, is the goal of life, for joy is the emotion which accompanies our fulfilling our natures as human beings. It is based on the experience of one's identity as a being of worth and dignity...

—Rollo May

Choose Life
Bernard Mandelbaum
Random House, NY, 1968

Remembered Joy

There are men who suffer terrible distress and are unable to tell what they feel in their hearts, and they go their way and suffer and suffer. But if they meet one with a laughing face, he can revive them with his joy. And to revive a man is no slight thing.

—Hasidic

Choose Life
Bernard Mandelbaum
New York: Random House, 1968

The Goal Is Joy

Dance and game are frivolous, unimportant down here; for "down here" is not their natural place. Here, they are a moment's rest from the life we were placed here to live. But in this world everything is upside down. That which, if it could be prolonged here, would be a truancy, is likest that which in a better country is the End of Ends. Joy is the serious business of Heaven.

—*C.S. Lewis*

The Joyful Christian
127 Readings from C.S. Lewis
Harper Collins Publishers, Ltd.

Grace Brings Joy

See, this kingdom of God is now found within us. The grace of the Holy Spirit shines forth and warms us, and overflowing with many and varied scents into the air around us, regales our senses with heavenly delight, as it fills our hearts with joy inexpressible.

—St. Seraphim of Sarov

Man and God
Victor Gollancz
Boston: Houghton Mifflin Co., 1951

Joyful Abandon

Joy, not grit, is the hallmark of holy obedience. We need to be lighthearted in what we do to avoid taking ourselves too seriously. It is a cheerful revolt against self and pride. Our work is jubilant, carefree, merry. Utter abandonment to God is done freely and with celebration.

—Richard J. Foster

Taken from "Joyful Abandon"
from *Freedom of Simplicity* by Richard J. Foster.
Copyright © 1981 by Richard J. Foster.
Reprinted by permission of HaperCollins Publishers, Inc.

Supernaturally Joyous

George Mueller would not preach until his heart was happy in the grace of God; Jan Ruysbroeck would not write while his feelings were low, but would retire to a quiet place and wait on God till he felt the spirit of inspiration. It is well known that the elevated spirits of a group of Moravians convinced John Wesley of the reality of their religion, and helped to bring him a short time later to a state of true conversion. The Christian owes it to the world to be supernaturally joyful.

—A. W. Tozer

Alliance Weekly

Shout for Joy!

*Shout for joy to the Lord,
all the earth.
Worship the Lord with gladness;
come before him with joyful songs.
Know that the Lord is God.*

—Psalm 100
HOLY BIBLE

Joy in the Morning

Weeping may endure for a night,
But joy comes in the morning.

—*Psalm 30:5*
HOLY BIBLE

Share It

Grief can take care of itself, but to get the full value of joy you must have somebody to divide it with.

—Mark Twain

The Book of Unusual Quotations
Selected and Edited by Rudolf Flesch
New York: Harper and Brothers Publishers, 1957

PEACE

In God's Hand

At the heart of the cyclone tearing the sky
And flinging the clouds and the towers by,
Is a place of central calm;
So here in the roar of mortal things,
I have a place where my spirit sings,
In the hollow of God's palm.

—Edwin Markham

A Treasury of Contentment
Complied and Edited by Ralph L. Woods
New York: Trident Press, 1969
A Division of Simon and Schuster

Called to Live in Peace

*If it is possible, as much as depends
on you, live peaceably with all men.*

—Romans 12:18

God has called us to peace.

—1 Corinthians 7:15

*And let the peace of God rule in your hearts, to which also you
were called in one body; and be thankful.*

—Colossians 3:14

HOLY BIBLE

His Peace

Jesus said:
Peace I leave with you,
my peace I give unto you:
not as the world giveth, give I unto you.
Let not your heart be troubled,
neither let it be afraid.

—John 14:27
HOLY BIBLE

Calm and Still

I take Thee for my Peace, O Lord,
My heart to keep and fill;
Thine own great calm, amid earth's storms,
Shall keep me always still,
And as Thy Kingdom doth increase,
So shall Thine ever-deepening peace.

—Annie W. Martson

Joy and Strength
Mary Wilder Tileston
Minnesota: World Wide Publications,
1901, 1929, 1986

Finding Rest in God

In comparison with this big world, the human heart is only a small thing. Though the world is so large, it is utterly unable to satisfy this tiny heart. The ever-growing soul and its capacity can be satisfied only by the infinite God. As water is restless until it reaches its level, so the soul has no peace until it rests in God.

—Sundar Singh

The Cross is Heaven:
The Life and Writings of Sadhu Sundar, 1957
Association Press

Pray for Peace

Do not be anxious about anything, but in everything, by prayer and petition, with thanksgiving, present your requests to God. And the peace of God, which transcends all understanding, will guard your hearts and your minds in Christ Jesus.

—Philippians 4:6-7 NIV

HOLY BIBLE

Peace

Were half the power that fills the world with terror,
Were half the wealth bestowed on camps and courts,
Given to redeem the human mind from error,
There were no need of arsenals or forts,

The warrior's name would be a name abhorr-d!
And every nation that should lift again
Its hand against a brother, on its forehead
Would wear for evermore the curse of Cain!

PEACE

Down the dark future, through long generations,
The echoing sounds grow fainter, and then cease;
And like a bell, with solemn, sweet vibrations,
I hear once more the voice of Christ say 'Peace!'

Peace! and no longer from its brazen portals
The blast of War's great organ shakes the skies!
But beautiful as songs of the immortals,
The holy melodies of love arise.

—H.W. Longfellow

Freedom, Love and Truth
William Inge
London: Longman, Green & Co., Inc., 1936

We Seek Peace

From his cradle to his grave a man never does a single thing which has any first and foremost object save one—to secure peace of mind, spiritual comfort, for himself.

—Mark Twain

The Book of Unusual Quotations
Selected and Edited by Rudolph Flesch
New York: Harper and Brothers Publishers, 1957

Collect for Peace

Most holy God, the source of all good desires, all right judgments, and all just works, give to us, Your servants, that peace which the world cannot give, so that our minds may be fixed on the doing of Your will, and that we, being delivered from the fear of all enemies, may live in peace and quietness; through the mercies of Christ Jesus our Savior. *Amen*

—Daily Evening Prayer

The Book of Common Prayer

Fall Silently

With that deep hush subduing all
Our words and works that drown
The tender whisper of Thy call,
As noiseless let Thy blessing fall
As fell the manna down.

—John G. Whittier

Joy and Strength
Mary Wilder Tileston
Minnesota: World Wide Publications
1901, 1929, 1986

Peace Is...

Peace is not an absence of war,
it is a virtue, a state of mind,
a disposition for benevolence,
confidence, justice.

—*Benedict Spinoza*

Harper's Quotations

Peace in the Midst

Two painters each painted a picture to illustrate his conception of rest. The first chose for his scene a still, lone lake among the far-off mountains.

The second threw on his canvas a thundering waterfall, with a fragile birch tree bending over the foam; and at the fork of the branch, almost wet with the cataract's spray, sat a robin on its nest.

The first was only *stagnation*; the last was *rest*.

Christ's life outwardly was one of the most troubled lives that ever lived: tempest and tumult, tumult and tempest, the waves breaking over it all the time until the worn body was laid in the grave. But the inner life was a sea of glass. The great calm was always there.

At any moment you might have gone to Him and found rest. And even when the human bloodhounds were dogging Him in the streets of Jerusalem, He turned to His disciples and offered them, as a last legacy, "My peace."

Rest is not a hallowed feeling that comes over us in church; it is the repose of a heart set deep in God.

—Drummond

Streams in the Desert
Compiled by Mrs. Charles E. Cowman
Los Angeles: Cowman Publications, Inc., 1959

Peacemakers

Peacemaking is a noble vocation. But you can no more make peace in your own strength than a mason can build a wall without a trowel, a carpenter build a house without a hammer, or an artist paint a picture without a brush. You must have the proper equipment. To be a peacemaker, you must know the Peace Giver. To make peace on earth, you must know the peace of heaven. You must know Him who "is our peace."

—Billy Graham

The Quotable Billy Graham
Compiled and Edited by Cort R. Flint and the Staff *Quote*
Anderson, S.C.: Droke House, 1966

Woven Together

Peace is the result of grace. It literally means, "To bind together." In other words, the peace which comes from unmerited, unearned love can weave and bind our fragmented lives into wholeness. And the civil war of divergent drives, which makes us feel like rubber bands stretched in all directions, is ended. The Lord is in control. He has forgiven the past, He is in charge of now, and shows the way for each new day.

—Lloyd John Ogilvie

Let God Love You, by Lloyd John Ogilvie
1974 by Word, Inc., Dallas, Texas.
All rights reserved.

False Peace

We have our peace movements, and all we want is peace—abroad and at home. But if by peace we mean appeasing tyranny, compromising with gangsters and being silent because we haven't the moral fortitude to speak out against injustice, then this is not real peace. It is a false peace. It is a farce and it is a hoax.

—Billy Graham

The Quotable Billy Graham
Compiled and Edited by Cort R. Flint and the Staff of *Quote*
Anderson, S.C.: Droke House, 1966

Diary of a Young Girl

I keep my ideals because in spite of everything I still believe that people are really good at heart. I simply can't build up my hopes on a foundation consisting of confusion, misery and death. I can feel the sufferings of millions, and yet, if I look up into the heavens, I think that it will come right, that this cruelty too will end, and that peace and tranquillity will return again.

—Anne Frank

Coming Day of Peace

"For thus says the Lord of hosts: 'Once more (it is a little while) I will shake heaven and earth, the sea and dry land; and I will shake all nations, and they shall come to the Desire of All Nations, and I will fill this temple with glory,' says the Lord of hosts. 'The silver is Mine, and the gold is Mine,' says the Lord of hosts. 'The glory of this latter temple shall be greater than the former,' says the Lord of hosts. 'And in this place I will give peace,' says the Lord of hosts."

—Haggai 2:6-9
HOLY BIBLE

PATIENCE

What is Patience?

"Longsuffering, bearing with one another in love."

—Ephesians 4:2
HOLY BIBLE

Not so in haste, my heart;
Have faith in God, and wait;
Although He linger long,
He never comes too late.

—Anonymous

Patience

I would submit to all Thy will,
For Thou art good and wise;
Let every anxious thought be still,
Nor one faint murmur rise.
Thy love can cheer the darksome gloom,
And bid me wait serene,
Till hopes and joys immortal bloom
And brighten all the scene.

Lincoln's Devotional
Greatneck, N.Y.: Channel Press, 1951

Surviving the Storm

There is no such thing as preaching patience into people unless the sermon is so long that they have to practice it while they hear. No man can learn patience except by going out into the hurly-burly world, and taking life just as it blows. Patience is but lying to and riding out the gale.

—Henry Ward Beecher

The New Dictionary of Thoughts
Originally Compiled by Tryon Edwards D.D.
Revised and Enlarged by C.N. Catrevas A.B.,
Jonathan Edwards A.M., & Ralph Emerson Browns A.M.
Standard Book Co., 1961

Locust Years

There are years in South Africa when locusts swarm the land and eat the crops. They come in hordes, blocking out the sun. The crops are lost and a hard winter follows. The "years that the locusts eat" are feared and dreaded. But the year after the locusts, South Africa reaps its greatest crops, for the dead bodies of the locusts serve as fertilizer for the new seed. And the locust year is restored as great crops swell the land.

This is a parable of our lives. There are seasons of deep distress and afflictions that sometimes eat all the usefulness of our lives away. Yet, the promise is that God will restore those locust years if we endure. We will reap if we faint not. Although now we do not know all the 'whys,' we can be assured our times are in His hands.

—Ron Hembree

Fruits of the Spirit
Grand Rapids, Mich.: Baker Book House, 1969

Increased Hope

Patience is not passive: on the contrary it is active; it is concentrated strength.

There is one form of hope which is never unwise, and which certainly does not diminish with the increase of knowledge. In that form it changes its name, and we call it patience.

—Bulwer

The New Dictionary of Thoughts
Originally Compiled by Tryon Edwards D.D.
Revised and Enlarged by C. N. Catrevas A. B.,
Jonathan Edwards A. M. Ralph Emerson Browns A. M.
Standard Book Co., 1961

Bundle Up

Patience serves as a protection against wrongs as clothes do against cold. For if you put on more clothes, as the cold increases it will have no power to hurt you. So in like manner you must grow in patience when you meet with great wrongs, and they will then be powerless to vex your mind.

—*Leonardo da Vinci*

The Book of Unusual Quotations
Selected and Edited by Rudolf Flesch
New York: Harper and Brothers Publishers, 1957

Teach Me, Lord, To Wait

Lord, to wait down on my knees
Till in Your own good time You answer my pleas;
Teach me not to rely on what others do,
But to wait in prayer for an answer from You.
They that wait upon the Lord shall renew their strength,
They shall mount up with wings as eagles;
They shall run and not be weary,
They shall walk and not faint.
Teach me, Lord, teach me, Lord, to wait.

—Stuart Hamblen

A Prayer of Patience

O blessed Lord, lead me whither Thou pleasest, I will follow Thee without complaint. I submit to Thy orders: I reverence thy wisdom: I trust myself with Thy goodness; I depend upon Thy almighty power: I rely on Thy promises; beseeching Thee to support me, till patience having its perfect working in me, I may be perfect, and entire, wanting nothing. I know the time is but short, and that Thou hast prepared long joys to recompense our momentary sorrows; help me, therefore, always to possess my soul in patience at present (giving thanks for the hope we have as an anchor of the soul both sure and steadfast) that so I may at last, after I have done Thy will, O God, inherit the promise. Amen.

—Evelyn Underhill

An Anthology of Devotional Literature
Compiled by Thomas S. Kepler
Grand Rapids, Mich.: Baker Book House, 1947

The Rarest Part

There's no music in a "rest," but there's the making of music in it. And people are always missing that part of the life melody, always talking of perseverance and courage and fortitude; but patience is the finest and worthiest part of fortitude, and the rarest, too.

—Ruskin

The New Dictionary of Thoughts
Originally compiled by Tryon Edwards D. D.
Revised and Enlarged by C. N. Catrevas A. B.,
Jonathan Edwards A. M., & Ralph Emerson Browns A. M.
Standard Book Co., 1961

Be Diligent

Have patience with all things, but chiefly have patience with yourself. Do not lose courage in considering your imperfections, but instantly set about remedying them—every day begin the task anew.

—*St. Francis de Sales*

The Book of Unusual Quotations
Selected and Edited by Rudolf Flesch
New York: Harper and Brothers Publishers, 1957

Concerning Patience

She is a Virtue, none can truly prize
Enough her Worth and Value, but the Wise
Who have her try'd, and her great Power known;
Her sublime Virtue, as th' admired Stone,
Brings things to pass, which some don't think to see,
Strange things to pass, hid in Obscurity;
Those that possess her in their Souls, shall know
Experience by her, deep things she will show:
But those that are impatient, and do fret,
The Night o'ertakes them, and their Sun doth set;
They cannot see far off, nor night at Hand;
The Light withdraws, and Darkness fills their Land.

—*Benjamin Antrobus*

Buds and Blossoms of Piety With Some Fruit
of the Spirit of Love and Directions to the Divine Wisdom
London, 1715

Running the Race

Let us lay aside every weight, and the sin which doth so easily beset us, and let us run with patience the race that is set before us,

Looking unto Jesus the author and finisher of our faith; who for the joy that was set before him endured the cross, despising the shame, and is set down at the right hand of the throne of God.

—Hebrews 12:1-2 KJV
HOLY BIBLE

Patience With a Smile

Be patient in little things. Learn to bear the everyday trials and annoyances of life quietly and calmly, and then, when unforeseen trouble or calamity comes, your strength will not forsake you. There is as much difference between genuine patience and sullen endurance, as between the smile of love, and the malicious gnashing of the teeth.

—William Swan Plumer

The New Dictionary of Thoughts
Originally Compiled by Tryon Edwards D. D.
Revised and Enlarged by C. N. Catrevas A.B., Jonathan Edwards A. M., & Ralph Emerson Browns A. M.
Standard Book Co., 1961

Make a Pearl

The most extraordinary thing about the oysters is this: Irritations get into his shell. He does not like them. But when he cannot get rid of them, he uses the irritation to do the loveliest thing an oyster ever has a chance to do. If there are irritations in our lives today, there is only one prescription: make a pearl. It may have to be a pearl of patience, but anyhow, make a pearl. And it takes faith and love to do it.

—Harry Emerson Fosdick

Reprinted with the permission of Simon & Schuster from *Words of Wisdom* by William Safire and Leonard Safire Copyright 1989 by Cobbett Corporation

We Must Be Tested

Patience does not mean indifference. We may work and trust and wait, but we ought not to be idle or careless while waiting.

Life has such hard conditions that every dear and precious gift, every rare virtue, every genial endowment, love, hope, joy, wit, sprightliness, benevolence, must sometimes be put into the crucible to distill the one elixir—patience.

—Gail Hamilton

The New Dictionary of Thoughts
Originally Compiled by Tryon Edwards D. D.
Revised and Enlarged by C. N. Catrevas A. B., Jonathan Edwards A. M. & Ralph Emerson Browns A. M.
Standard Book Co., 1961

KINDNESS

A Father's Kindness

Busy in his study a minister was preparing his sermon for the coming Sunday. He reached to the shelf at his side for a book, and then remembered that he had left it downstairs. His little daughter was playing in the bedroom, and he called her. She came, running, eager and delighted at the thought that Papa needed her. He explained carefully where she could find the book, and she went gladly, returning in a moment with a book which he saw at a

glance was the wrong one. But he hardly looked at the book as he took it and laid it on the table. He looked only at the eager face of his little daughter, wreathed in smiles. Gathering her close to his heart, he kissed her and said, "Thank you, darling." And when she had gone back happy and contented to her play he went quietly for the book he needed. I think I should like to listen to the sermons that man would preach.

Christian Herald

Cyclopedia of Religious Anecdotes
Compiled by James Gilchrist Lawson
Fleming H. Revell Co., 1923

You're Not God

Has God deserted Heaven,
And left it up to you,
To judge if this or that is right,
And what each one should do?
I think He's still in business,
And knows when to wield the rod,
So when you're judging others,
Just remember, you're not—God.

Pass It On

Have you had a kindness shown?
Pass it on;
'Twas not given for thee alone,
Pass it on;
Let it travel down the years,
Let it wipe another's tears,
'Till in Heaven the deed appears—
Pass it on.

—Henry Burton

The Encyclopedia of Religious Quotations
Edited and Compiled by Frank S. Mead
Fleming H. Revell, 1965

Cheer the Lonely Heart

I remember hearing of a man in one of the hospitals who received a bouquet of flowers from the Flower Mission. He looked at the beautiful bouquet and said, "Well, if I had known that a bunch of flowers could do a fellow so much good, I would have sent some myself when I was well." If people only knew how they might cheer some lonely heart and lift up some drooping spirit, or speak some word that shall be lasting in its effects for all coming time, they would be up and about it.

—Dwight L. Moody

The D. L. Moody Year Book
Selected by Emma Moody Fitt
New York: Fleming H. Revell, 1900

Words of Kindness

Kind words bring no blisters on the tongue that speaks them, nor on the ear which hears them. Kind words are never wasted. Like scattered seeds, they spring up in unexpected places. Kindness is a conquering weapon. Kindness should not be all on one side. One good turn must have another as its return, or it will not be fair. He who expects kindness should show kindness.

—*C. H. Spurgeon*

Spurgeon's Proverbs and Sayings With Notes Vol. I
Grand Rapids, Mich.: Baker Book House

Soothing Words

Kind words produce their own image in men's souls; and a beautiful image it is. They soothe and quiet and comfort the hearer. They shame him out of his sour, morose, unkind feelings. We have not yet begun to use kind words in such abundance as they ought to be used.

—*Blaise Pascal*

The New Dictionary of Thoughts
Originally Compiled by Tryon Edwards D.D.
Revised and Enlarged by C. N. Catrevas A. B., Jonathan Edwards A. M. & Ralph Emerson Browns A. M.
Standard Book Co., 1961

Kindness Leads to Friendship

We cannot tell the precise moment when friendship is formed. As in filling a vessel drop by drop, there is at last a drop which makes it run over; so in a series of kindnesses there is at last one which makes the heart run over.

—James Boswell

Barlett's Familiar Quotations, 16th Edition
John Barlett
Justin Kaplan, General Editor
Boston: Little, Brown & Co., 1992

Anyone Can Do It

The ministry of kindness is a ministry which may be achieved by all men, rich and poor, learned and illiterate. Brilliance of mind and capacity for deep thinking have rendered great service to humanity, but by themselves they are impotent to dry a tear or mend a broken heart.

—Anonymous

The Encyclopedia of Religious Quotations
Edited and Compiled by Frank S. Mead
Fleming H. Revell, 1965

Small Kindnesses Add Up

Life is made up, not of great sacrifices or duties, but of little things, in which smiles, and kindnesses, and small obligations, given habitually, are what win and preserve the heart and secure comfort.

—Sir H. Davy

The New Dictionary of Thoughts
Originally Compiled by Tryon Edwards D. D.
Revised and Enlarged by C. N. Catrevas A. B., Jonathan Edwards A. M. & Ralph Emerson Browns A. M.
Standard Book Co., 1961

His Kindness Is Better Than Life

O God, You are my God;
Early will I seek You;
My soul thirsts for You;
My flesh longs for You
In a dry and thirsty land
Where there is no water.
So I have looked for You in the sanctuary,
To see Your power and Your glory.

KINDNESS

Because Your lovingkindness is better than life,
My lips shall praise You.
Thus I will bless You while I live;
I will lift up my hands in your name.
My soul shall be satisfied as with marrow and fatness,
And my mouth shall praise You with joyful lips.

—Psalm 63:1-5

HOLY BIBLE

An Unpredictable Kindness

In contrast to revenge, which is the natural, automatic reaction to transgression and which, because of the irreversibility of the action process, can be expected and even calculated, the act of forgiving can never be predicted; it is the only reaction that acts in an unexpected way and thus retains, through being a reaction, something of the original character of action.

—Hannah Arendt

The Worst Disease

I have come more and more to realize that being unwanted is the worst disease that any human being can ever experience.

Nowadays we have found medicine for leprosy, and lepers can be cured. There's medicine for TB, and consumption can be cured. But for being unwanted, except there are willing hands to serve and there's a loving heart to love, I don't think this terrible disease can be cured.

—Mother Teresa

Reprinted from *Peacemaking: Day by Day*
by Mother Teresa of India.
Copyright by PAX Christi USA.
Used by permission of PAX Christi USA, National Catholic Peace Movement

Christian Community

The second service that one should perform for another in a Christian community is that of active helpfulness. This means, initially, simple assistance in trifling, external matters. There is a multitude of these things wherever people live together. Nobody is too good for the meanest service. One who worries about the loss of time that such petty, outward acts of helpfulness entail is usually taking the importance of his own career too solemnly.

—Dietrich Bonhoeffer

Taken from *Life Together* by Dietrich Bonhoeffer.
English translation copyright © 1954 by Harper & Brothers,
copyright renewed © 1982 by Helen S. Doberstein.
Reprinted by permission of HarperCollins Publishers, Inc.

Receiving and Giving

What makes the Dead Sea dead? Because it is all the time receiving, but never giving out anything. Why is it that many Christians are cold? Because they are all the time receiving, never giving out.

—Dwight L. Moody

The D. L. Moody Year Book
Selected by Emma Moody Fitt
New York: Fleming H. Revell, 1900

Do What I Can

If I can stop one heart from breaking,
I shall not live in vain:
If I can ease one life the aching,
Or cool one pain,
Or help one fainting robin
Unto his nest again,
I shall not live in vain.

—*Emily Dickinson*

One Hundrend and One Famous Poems
An Anthology Compiled by Roy J. Cook
Chicago: Contemporary Books, Inc., 1958

GOODNESS

Degrees of Giving

A Spanish scholar of the twelfth century, Moses Maimonides, depicts seven steps in what he calls the ladder of charity and giving: The first and lowest degree is to give, but with reluctance. The second is to give cheerfully, but not in proportion to the distress of the sufferer. The third step is to give cheerfully and proportionately, but not until solicited. The fourth is to give cheerfully, proportionately and unsolicitedly, but yourself to put the gift in the poor man's hand, thus exciting in him the painful emotion of shame. The fifth is to know the object of your bounty, but to remain unknown to him. The sixth is to bestow charity in such a way that the benefactor may not know the recipient, nor the recipient his benefactor. The seventh and worthiest step is to anticipate charity by preventing poverty. This is the highest step and summit of charity's golden ladder.

—Paul S. McElroy

Quiet Thoughts
Mount Vernon, N.Y.: Peter Pauper Press

Love At Work

Goodness is love in action, love with its hand to the plow, love with the burden on its back, love following His footsteps who went about continually doing good.

—James Hamilton

The Encyclopedia of Religious Quotations
Edited and Compiled by Frank S. Mead
Fleming H. Revell Co., 1965

The Godly Eye

"The lamp of the body is the eye; if therefore your eye is clear, your whole body will be full of light.

"But if your eye is bad, your whole body will be full of darkness. If therefore the light that is in you is darkness, how great is the darkness!"

—Matthew 6:22-23 NASB
HOLY BIBLE

Stars Still Shine

Were a star quenched on high,
For ages would its light,
Still traveling downward from the sky,
Shine on our mortal sight.
So when a great man dies,
For years beyond our ken,
The light he leaves behind him lies
Upon the paths of men.

—Henry Wadsworth Longfellow

Being Made Good

The spirit makes war on all that is poor, shoddy, showy; weaves the different threads of personality into good material, real hard-wearing solid stuff—and not only in the sphere of behaviour or devotion. It makes human beings into fully living men, not through their own efforts and strivings, but by the penetration of God.

—Evelyn Underhill

The Fruits of the Spirit
London: Longman, House., 1949

Good Works

The Christian is in a different position from other people who are trying to be good. They hope, by being good, to please God if there is one; or—if they think there is not—at least they hope to deserve approval from good men. But the Christian thinks any good he does comes from the Christ-life inside him. He does not think God will love us because we are good, but that God will make us good because He loves us.

—*C. S. Lewis*

Mere Christianity
HarperCollins Ltd.

No Exchanges

Wherever a man hath been made a partaker of the divine nature, in him is fulfilled the best and noblest life, and the worthiest in God's eyes, that hath been or can be. And of that eternal love which loveth Goodness as Goodness and for the sake of Goodness, a true, noble, Christ-like life is so greatly beloved that it will never be forsaken or cast off. Where a man hath tasted this life, it is impossible for him ever to part with it...and if he could exchange it for an angel's life, he would not.

—Theologia Germanica

Overcome Evil With Good

Beloved, do not avenge yourselves, but rather give place to wrath; for it is written, "'Vengeance is Mine, I will repay,' says the Lord.

Therefore "If your enemy is hungry, feed him; If he is thirsty, give him a drink; For in so doing you will heap coals of fire on his head."

Do not be overcome by evil, but overcome evil with good.

—Romans 12:19-21
HOLY BIBLE

The Father's Goodness

The Father was all in all to the Son, and the Son no more thought of His own goodness than an honest man thinks of his honesty. When the good man sees goodness, he thinks of his own evil: Jesus had no evil to think of, but neither does He think of His goodness: He delights in His Father's. "Why callest thou Me good?"

—George MacDonald

Unspoken Sermons
Second Series, The Way
George MacDonald, 365 Readings
Edited by C.S. Lewis
New York: Macmillan, 1947

Salvation's Cost

The story is told of a hero of the Chinese rice-fields during an earthquake. From his hilltop farm he saw the ocean swiftly withdrawn, like some prodigious animal crouching for the leap, and knew the leap would be the tidal wave. He saw also that his neighbors working in low fields must be gathered to his hill or swept away. Without a second thought he set fire to his rice-ricks and furiously rang the temple-bell. His neighbors thought his farm on fire and rushed to help him. Then, from that safe hill they saw the swirl of waters over fields just forsaken—and knew their salvation and its cost.

—*Lafcadio Hearn*

Thesaurus of Anecdotes
Edited by Edmund Fuller
New York: Crown Publishers, 1942

Don't Be Selfish

Goodness is something so simple; always to live for others, never to seek one's own advantage.

—*Dag Hammarskjöld*

Choose Life
Bernard Mandelbum
New York: Random House, 1968

Signpost

Real goodness does not attach itself merely to this life — it points to another world. Political or professional reputation cannot last forever, but a conscience void of offence before God and man is an inheritance for eternity.

—Daniel Webster

The Encyclopedia of Religious Quotations
Edited and Compiled by Frank S. Mead
Fleming H. Revell Co., 1965

Always There

The Lord's goodness surrounds us at every moment. I walk through it almost with difficulty, as through thick grass and flowers.

—R.W. Barbour

A Diary of Readings
John Baillie
New York: Collier Books/Macmillan, 1955, 1986

God's Nature

Since His goodness is so great, His will so perfect, that He does what ought to be done, not unwilling, but spontaneously, He is so much the more completely to be loved because of His very nature, and the more to be glorified because this goodness of His belongs to Him not by accident, but substantially and immutably.

—*Pierre Abelard*

Epitome Theologiae Christianne, c. 1135
The World Treasury of Religious Quotations
Compiled and Edited by Ralph L. Woods
New York: Hawthorn Boos, Inc., 1966

FAITHFULNESS

For All Time

In God's faithfulness lies
eternal security.

—Corrie ten Boom

Encyclopedia of Famous Quotes

Believe...See

Faith is to believe what we do not see, and the reward of this faith is to see what we believe.

—St. Augustine

Cyclopedia of Religious Anecdotes

Step of Faith

Whoso draws nigh to God one step
through doubtings dim,
God will advance a mile
in blazing light to Him.

—Anonymous

Mind Your Place

Is your place a small place?
Tend it with care!—He set you there.
Is your place a large place?
Guard it with care!—He set you there.
Whate'er your place, it is
Not yours alone, but His
Who set you there.

—*John Oxenham (1861-1941)*

Hidden Heroes

John Egglen had never preached a sermon in his life. Never. Wasn't that he didn't want to, just never needed to. But then one morning he did. The snow left his town of Colchester, England, buried in white. When he awoke on that January Sunday in 1850, he thought of staying home. Who would go to church in such weather? But he reconsidered. He was, after all, a deacon. And if the deacons didn't go, who would? So he put on his boots, hat, and coat and walked the six miles to the Methodist Church. He wasn't the only member who considered staying home. In fact, he was one of the few who came. Only thirteen people were present. Twelve members and one visitor. Even the minister was snowed in. Someone suggested they go home. Egglen would hear none of that. They'd come this far; they would have a service. Besides, they had a visitor. A thirteen-year-old boy.

But who would preach? Egglen was the only deacon. It fell to him. And so he did. His sermon lasted only ten minutes. It drifted and wandered and made no point in an effort to make several. But at the end, an uncharacteristic courage settled upon the man. He lifted his eyes and looked straight at the boy and challenged: "Young man, look to Jesus. Look! Look! Look!" Did the challenge make a difference? Let the boy, now a man, answer. "I did look, and then and there the cloud on my heart lifted, the darkness rolled away, and at that moment I saw the sun." The boy's name? Charles Haddon Spurgeon. England's prince of preachers.

—Max Lucado

When God Whispers Your Name
Dallas: Word Publishing, 1994

Where Faithfulness Leads

Don't expect wisdom to come into your life like great chunks of rock on a conveyor belt. It isn't like that. It's not splashy and bold...nor is it dispensed like a prescription across a counter. Wisdom comes privately from God as a by-product of right decisions, godly reactions, and the application of spiritual principles to daily circumstances. Wisdom comes...not from trying to do great things for God...but more from being faithful to the small, obscure tasks few people ever see.

—Charles R. Swindoll

Encyclopedia of Famous Quotes

Faith Is of the Heart

The heart has its reasons of which reason knows nothing. We feel it in a thousand things. I say that the heart naturally loves the Universal Being, and naturally loves itself; and it gives itself to one or the other, and hardens itself against one or the other, as it chooses...It is the heart that feels God, not the reason; this is faith.

—*Blaise Pascal*

Eerdmans' Book of Christian Classics
Compiled by Veronica Zundel
Grand Rapids, Mich.: William B. Eerdmans Publishing Company, 1985

God's Heroes

To fill a little space because God wills it; to go on cheerfully with the petty round of little duties, little avocations; to accept unmurmuringly a low position; to be misunderstood, misrepresented, maligned, without complaint, to smile for the joys of others when the heart is aching; to banish all ambition, all pride, and all restlessness, in a single regard to our Savior's work; he who does this is a greater hero than he who for one hour storms a beach, or for one day rushes onward undaunted in the flaming front of shot and shell. His works will follow him. He may be no hero to the world, but he is one of God's heroes.

—F.W. Faber

Treasure Thoughts
F.W. Faber
Edited by Rose Porter

God Can Use Our Mistakes

I believe that God can and will bring good out of evil, even out of the greatest evil. For that purpose he needs men who make the best use of everything. I believe that God will give us all the strength we need to help us resist in all time of distress. But he never gives it in advance, lest we should rely on ourselves and not on Him alone. A faith such as this should allay all our fears for the future. I believe that even our mistakes and shortcomings are turned to good account, and that is no harder for God to deal with them than with our supposedly good deeds. I believe that God is no timeless fate, but that He waits for and answers sincere prayers and responsible actions.

—Dietrich Bonhoeffer

Reprinted with the permission of Simon & Schuster from
Letters and Papers from Prison: Revised, Enlarged Edition.
Copyright © 1953,1967,1971 by SCM Press, Ltd.

Always There

Almighty God is on our team. He is our faithful Sustainer. When everybody else abandons us, we can count on Him. When nobody else is willing to endure with us, He is there. He is trustworthy, reliable, and consistent. We can depend upon Him.

—Charles Stanley

How to Listen to God
Nashville: Thomas Nelson, 1985

The Right Call

God has not called me to be successful;
he has called me to be faithful.

—Mother Teresa

Encyclopedia of Famous Quotes

Solid Ground

Here in the maddening maze of times
When tossed by storm and flood
To one fixed ground my spirit clings
I know that God is good.

Another Tassel Is Moved
Louis O. Caldwell
Grand Rapids, Mich.: Baker Book House

GENTLENESS

Under Control

The word "gentleness" here (or in the KJV, meekness) comes from a Greek word meaning "mild; mildness in dealing with others." Jesus said, *"Blessed are the gentle, for they shall inherit the earth"* (Matthew 5:5 NASB). Nowhere in Scripture does this word carry with it the idea of being spiritless and timid. In biblical times, gentleness or meekness meant far more than it does in modern-day English. It carried the idea of being tamed, like a wild horse that has been brought under control.

Gentle Truth

A missionary in Jamaica asked a boy this question, "Who are the meek?"

The boy answered, "Those who give soft answers to rough questions."

—Unknown

He's Right

Since the Bible puts a premium on meekness, I must cultivate it. Meekness is not weakness, as many have pointed out, but in the words of a Christian brother, "Meekness is 'I accept God's dealings with me without bitterness.'" Meekness says God is always right. I must always accept what He sends me, and I must always do it with gladness of heart.

—W. Glyn Evans

Daily With the King
Chicago: Moody Press, 1979

Anything But

Meekness is not weakness.

—*Sir William Gurney Benham*

Encyclopedia of Famous Quotes

In Control

The meek are not those who are never at all angry, for such are insensible; but those who, feeling anger, control it, and are angry only when they ought to be. Meekness excludes revenge, irritability, morbid sensitiveness, but not self-defence, or a quiet and steady maintenance of right.

—Theophylactus

The International Dictionary of Thoughts
Edited by Bradley, Daniels & Jones
Doubleday & Co., 1969

By Definition

It is almost a definition of a gentleman to say that he is one who never inflicts pain.

—*Captain John Henry Newman*

The Idea of A University
Knowledge and Religious Duty, 1852

The Face of Humility

Except in faith, nobody is humble. The mask of weakness or of Phariseeism is not the naked face of humility.

And, except in faith, nobody is proud. The vanity displayed in all its varieties by the spiritually immature is not pride.

To be, in faith, both humble and proud: this is, to live, to know that in God I am nothing, but that God is in me.

—Dag Hammarskjöld

From *Markings* by Dag Hammarskjöld, trans.,
Leif Sjoberg & W.H. Auden
Translation copyright © 1964 by Alfred A. Knopf Inc. and Faber Ltd.
Reprinted by permission of Alfred A. Knopf.
New York: Alfred A. Knopf, 1964

Gentleness Makes Great

Thou hast also given me the shield of thy salvation: and thy right hand hath holden me up, and thy gentleness hath made me great.

—*Psalm 18:35* KJV

HOLY BIBLE

Gentle With the Opposition

A servant of the Lord must not quarrel but be gentle to all, able to teach, patient, in humility correcting those who are in opposition, if God perhaps will grant them repentance, so that they may know the truth, and that they may come to their senses and escape the snare of the devil, having been taken captive by him to do his will.

—2 Timothy 2:24-26
HOLY BIBLE

Inner Beauty

Your beauty should not come from outward adornment, such as braided hair and the wearing of gold jewelry and fine clothes. Instead, it should be that of your inner self, the unfading beauty of a gentle and quiet spirit, which is of great worth in God's sight. For this is the way the holy women of the past who put their hope in God used to make themselves beautiful.

—1 Peter 3:3-5 NIV
HOLY BIBLE

Gentle

The word gentle was rarely heard before the Christian era, and the word gentleman was not known. This high quality of character was a direct by-product of Christian faith.

—Billy Graham

The Quotable Billy Graham
Compiled and Edited by Cort R. Flint and the Staff of *Quote*
Anderson, S.C.: Droke House, 1966

Be Humble

There is no true and constant gentleness without humility. While we are so fond of ourselves, we are easily offended with others. Let us be persuaded that nothing is due to us, and then nothing will disturb us. Let us often think of our own infirmities, as we shall become indulgent toward those of others.

—Fenelon

Daily Strength for Daily Needs
Mary Tileston

Moving, Yet Still

Meekness is imperfect if it be not both active and passive, leading us to subdue our own passions and resentments, as well as to bear patiently the passions and resentments of others.

—John Watson Foster

International Dictionary of Thoughts
Doubleday and Company, 1969

Choosing Gentleness

Nothing is won by force. I choose to be gentle. If I raise my voice may it be only in praise. If I clench my fist, may it be only in prayer. If I make a demand, may it be only of myself.

—Max Lucado

When God Whispers Your Name
Dallas: Word Inc., 1994

Worthy

Walk worthy of the vocation wherewith ye are called, with all lowliness and meekness, with longsuffering, forbearing one another in love.

—Ephesians 4:1-2 KJV

Meekness, humility, and love,
Did through thy conduct shine;
Oh may my whole deportment prove
A copy, Lord, of Thine.

Lincoln's Devotional
Greatneck, N.Y.: Channel Press, Inc., 1957

SELF-CONTROL

An End to Troubles

Cry for grace from God to be able to see God's hand in every trial, and then for grace...to submit at once to it. Not only to submit, but to acquiesce, and to rejoice in it...I think there is generally an end to troubles when we get to that.

—Charles H. Spurgeon

Power in Praise
Merlin Carothers
Plainfield, N.J.: Logos International, 1971

Indispensable

If a person mounts a high-spirited horse, it is important that he should be able to control him; otherwise he may be dashed in pieces. If an engineer undertakes to conduct a locomotive, it is necessary that he should be able to guide or check the panting engine at his pleasure; else his own life and the lives of others may be sacrificed. But it is still more indispensable that an individual who is entrusted with the care of himself should be able to govern himself.

—S.G. Goodrich

6000 Illustrations

Let Dogs Delight to Bark and Bite

Let dogs delight to bark and bite,
  For God hath made them so;
Let bears and lions grow and fight,
  For 'tis their nature too.

But, children, you should never let
  Such angry passions rise;
Your little hands were never made
  To tear each other's eyes.

—*Isaac Watts*

Worthwhile Work

Thank God every morning when you get up that you have something to do that day which must be done, whether you like it or not. Being forced to work, and forced to do your best will breed in you temperance and self-control, diligence and strength of will, cheerfulness and content, and a hundred virtues which the idle will never know.

—Charles Kingsley

A Treasury of Contentment
Complied and Edited by Ralph L. Woods
New York: Trident Press, 1969
A Division of Simon and Schuster

Temperance

Take heed to yourselves, lest at any time your hearts be overcharged with surfeiting, and drunkenness, and cares of this life, and so that day come upon you unawares.

—Luke 21:34 KJV

The world employs its various snares,
Of hopes and pleasures, pains and cares,
And chain'd to earth I lie:
When shall my fetter'd powers be free,
And leave these seats of vanity,
And upward learn to fly?

Lincoln's Devotional
Introduction by Carl Sandburg
Greatneck, N.Y.: Channel Press, Inc., 1957

The Choice

I choose self-control...

I am a spiritual being. After this body is dead, my spirit will soar. I refuse to let what will rot, rule the eternal. I choose self-control. I will be drunk only by joy. I will be impassioned only by my faith. I will be influenced only by God. I will be taught only by Christ. I choose self-control.

—*Max Lucado*

When God Whispers Your Name
Dallas: Word Inc., 1994

True Royalty

The command of one's self is the greatest empire a man can aspire unto, and consequently, to be subject to our own passions is the most grievous slavery. He who best governs himself is best fitted to govern others. He who reigns within himself and rules his passions, desires and fears is more than a king.

—John Milton

The New Dictionary of Thoughts
Originally Compiled by Tryon Edwards D.D.
Revised and enlarged by C.N. Catrevas A.B.,
Jonathan Edwards A.M. & Ralph Emerson Browns A.M.
Standard Book Co., 1961

It Takes Time

Willpower, (Nick Lansing) saw, was not a thing one could suddenly decree oneself to possess. It must be built up imperceptibly and laboriously out of a succession of small efforts to meet definite objects, out of the facing of daily difficulties instead of cleverly eluding them or shifting their burden on others. The making of the substance called character was a process about as slow and arduous as the building of the Pyramids.

—Edith Wharton

The Glimpses of the Moon

Silent Before His Accusers

Now Jesus stood before the governor; and the governor questioned Him, saying, "Are You the King of the Jews?" And Jesus said to him, "It is as you say."

And while He was being accused by the chief priests and elders, He made no answer.

Then Pilate said to Him, "Do You not hear how many things they testify against You?"

And He did not answer him with regard to even a single charge, so that the governor was quite amazed.

—Matthew 27:11-14 NASB
HOLY BIBLE

Non-Sense

Temperance is not the absence of passion but is the transfiguring of passion into wholeness. Without it...you will have the senses usurping sovereignty and excluding the spirit; you will have them deciding good and evil and excluding God.

—Gerald Vann

The Heart of Man, 1945

Balance

We have to acquire a peace and balance of mind such that we can give every word of criticism its due weight, and humble ourselves before every word of praise.

—Dag Hammarskjöld

From *Markings* by Dag Hammarskjöld, trans.,
Leif Sjoberg & W.H. Auden.
Translation copyright © by Alfred A. Knopf Inc. Faber and Faber Ltd.
Reprinted by permission of Alfred A. Knopf Inc.
New York: Alfred A. Knopf, 1964

Some Or None

Temperance is a moderation in the things that are good and total abstinence from the things that are foul.

—Frances E. Willard

The Encyclopedia of Religious Quotations
Edited and Compiled by Frank S. Mead
Fleming H. Revell Co., 1965

Keeping Your Temper

Let your light so shine before men, that they may see your good works, and glorify your Father which is in heaven.

—Matthew 5:16 KJV

If a man has not grace to keep his temper, he is not fit to work for God. If he cannot live uprightly at home, he is not fit for God's service; and the less he does the better. But he can keep his temper, he can live uprightly at home, by the grace of God.

—D.L. Moody

The D.L. Moody Year Book
Selected by Emma Moody Fitt
New York: Fleming H. Revell, 1900

Holding Your Tongue

He that covereth a transgression seeketh love;
but he that repeateth a matter separateth very friends.
—Proverbs 17:9 KJV

"Covering a transgression" simply means that we don't spout off about everything we know of a wrong inflicted. At times, it means "just don't bring it up at all." But there is more: God says that if we remain silent under these conditions, then He knows that we are truly seeking love. Love is far different from the tempting thrill of shocking someone with a bit of sensational news. Love covers. Love protects. Love endures the boredom, often dullness, of just keeping still.

—Eugenia Price

From *Another Day* by Eugenia Price.
Copyright © 1984 by Eugenia Price.
Used by permission of Doubleday, a division of Bantam Doubleday Dell Publishing Group, Inc.

Firm Control

There must be firm control of the sex impulse. This God-given instinct has been dragged through the gutter by modern thinking, and we have made a cheap toy out of the most sacred gifts God has ever given to man. Our pro-creative powers need to be dedicated to Christ.

—Billy Graham

The Quotable Billy Graham
Compiled and Edited by Cort R. Flint and the Staff of *Quote*
Anderson, S.C.: Droke House, 1966

My Kingdom

A little kingdom I possess,
Where thoughts and feelings dwell;
And very hard the task I find
Of governing it well...
I do not ask for any crown
But that which all may win;
Nor try to conquer any world
Except the one within.

—*Louisa May Alcott*

Other Titles by Honor Books

God's Treasury of Virtues
God's Little Instruction Book on Prayer
God's Little Instruction Book on Love
God's Little Instruction Book on Friendship
God's Little Instruction Book on Success
God's Little Instruction Book on Character
John Wesley's Little Instruction Book
Martin Luther's Little Instruction Book
Dwight L. Moody's Little Instruction Book